A is for Asian American

An Asian Pacific Islander Desi American Alphabet

By Virginia Loh-Hagan • Illustrated by Tracy Nishimura Bishop

PUBLISHED BY SLEEPING BEAR PRESS

I am an Asian American. My cultural history blends Chinese, Cambodian, and American traditions. I come from a family of immigrants and refugees. I know what it's like to feel cultural pride. I feel it when I see people who look like me in movies, books, and school curricula. I also know what it's like to feel different, to feel like you don't belong. In 2020 during the COVID-19 pandemic, there was an increase in anti-Asian hate. This made me feel sad. I found comfort and safety in the community groups that stood in solidarity against hate. I also found peace in writing books like this. We need more books and movies about Asian Pacific Islander Desi American (APIDA) history and experiences. We need to learn more so that we can do more. Let's be better together!

—Virginia Loh-Hagan

Little-Known Milestones You Need to Know

The following are some significant APIDA moments in US history that you probably did not learn in school and that are not featured in this book. I have presented a few notable milestones but there are so many other highlights and achievements to celebrate in the APIDA community. Everyone should care about APIDA history. Know APIDA history so that you can better know yourself.

Milestones in Early Immigration History

1763 Filipinos established the first Asian American settlement in the bayous of Louisiana. They were called "Manilamen" and married Cajun and Native American women.

1841 A 14-year-old fisherman named Manjirō became the first official United States Japanese immigrant. He was adopted by American Captain William Whitfield who rescued Manjirō from a shipwreck off Japan's coast.

1884 The first Koreans, mainly politicians and students, arrived in the United States. Philip Jaisohn, a political activist and doctor, was the first Korean naturalized citizen of the United States.

1898 Spain ceded the island of Guam to the United States. This started a migration of Chamorros, the indigenous people living in Guam, to California and Hawai'i.

Milestones in the APIDA Social Justice Movement

1885 The Supreme Court of California ruled in favor of Mamie Tape, an 8-year-old Chinese American. It ensured that minority children had a right to attend the state's public schools.

1923 Bhagat Singh Thind fought for Indian immigrants to be naturalized citizens. He lost his case in the US Supreme Court. He applied again in 1936. As a World War I veteran, he was finally granted citizenship.

1993 The first Onipa'a Peace March was held. This march commemorated the 100th anniversary of the illegal overthrow of the kingdom of Hawai'i and promoted Hawaiian rights and independence.

2021 By making a viral video calling for more media attention, Amanda Nguyen, a Vietnamese American, kickstarted the movement to stop violence against Asian Americans. She is also a women's rights activist.

Milestones in Innovation

1920s Pedro Flores, a Filipino American immigrant, made yo-yos popular in the United States. He invented a loop design that enabled yo-yos to do tricks.

1950 Isabella Aiona Abbott was the first native Hawaiian woman to earn a doctorate in science. She studied Hawaiian seaweeds. She discovered more than 200 species. She also created recipes using seaweed.

1997 Kalpana Chawla, an Indian American, was the first Indian-born woman to go to space. She spent a total of 30 days, 14 hours, and 54 minutes in space. She operated the space shuttle's robotic arm.

2011 Eric Yuan, a Chinese American, invented the Zoom video-conferencing platform. During the COVID-19 pandemic, Zoom was widely used as people shifted from in-person to online meetings.

Milestones in Pop Culture

1937 Gobind Behari Lal became the first Indian American to win the Pulitzer Prize. He was the first journalist to describe himself as a "science writer."

1970s –1980s Asian American musicians created their own distinct genre of music known as Asian American jazz. Asian instruments were used along with standard jazz instruments.

2012 Linsanity began. Jeremy Lin was the first Taiwanese American to play in the National Basketball Association (NBA). He was the first Asian American to win a championship. He gained many fans when he kicked off a winning streak for the New York Knicks.

2020 Awkwafina, a rapper and actress, was the first Asian American to win the Golden Globe Award for Best Actress. She won for performing in *The Farewell*.

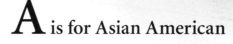

A is for Asian American

Asian Americans and Pacific Islanders
have roots across the sea.
They're also an important
part of US history.

Asian Americans are people with Asian ancestry. They include people from Asia and the Pacific Islands. Asia is the largest continent with more than 40 countries, more than 2,000 spoken languages, and hundreds of ethnic groups. Far East Asia includes China, Japan, and Korea. Southeast Asia includes Vietnam, Thailand, and Cambodia. South Asia includes India, Pakistan, and Bangladesh. (Some people with South Asian backgrounds call themselves Desi Americans.) Asian Americans also include people from Mongolia and Central Asia.

The Pacific Islands consist of thousands of islands in the Pacific Ocean, including Fiji and Samoa. The Philippines is in the Pacific Ocean, but some consider it to be part of Southeast Asia.

Asian Americans have very unique cultures, histories, and languages. Early Asian immigrants were known by their specific ethnicities, such as Chinese American. This changed in the 1960s, when activists Emma Gee and Yuji Ichioka organized to fight for equal rights. They used the term "Asian American" to bring together groups of people from different Asian backgrounds. They were inspired by the African American civil rights movement.

B is for Beautiful Country

By building the railroads,
Chinese workers opened the west.
Yet they had to fight to stay
and not be seen as unwanted guests.

The Chinese word for the United States means "Beautiful Country." Chinese laborers arrived in the 1850s when gold was found in California. They were the first large Asian immigrant group to settle in the United States. Smaller groups of Japanese and Filipino laborers also arrived in Hawai'i and California.

Chinese immigrants found work mining for gold or building the Transcontinental Railroad, which was completed in 1869. Some returned to China, but many settled in the United States. Many white Americans saw Chinese immigrants as a threat, accusing them of taking away their jobs. In 1882, the United States passed a law excluding Chinese workers from immigrating. This led to Chinese immigrants being stopped and questioned at the Angel Island Immigration Station, which opened in 1910, in San Francisco Bay. Many were denied admission and deported back to China.

There were big changes in immigration laws in the 1960s. This resulted in an increase of highly educated and skilled Asian immigrants. In the 1970s, wars in Southeast Asia resulted in many Southeast Asians immigrating to the United States as refugees.

Bb

Cc

C is for Communities

Asian immigrants built
their own lively spaces.
They created little towns
that felt like their birthplaces.

Early Chinese immigrants needed a place to live while they worked. But they weren't allowed to live in certain parts of a town. In some cases, they were driven out of areas where white people lived. So they created their own spaces within these towns.

The first Chinatown sprang up in San Francisco, California, which was a port of entry for early Chinese immigrants in the 1850s. More Chinatowns popped up along the West Coast. As railroads were being built, Chinatowns were formed in railroad towns. They also formed on the East Coast, where Chinese immigrants worked in factories and other businesses that needed cheap labor.

As more Asian immigrants arrived, other ethnic communities were developed. For example, there are Koreatowns, Little Indias, Little Tokyos, Manilatowns, Asiatowns, etc. These communities are usually in urban areas. They provided safety and community to Asian immigrants. Residents organized themselves. They set up businesses, provided services, and created their own political leadership. Today these communities are centers for tourism. They're often seen as the pride of major cities.

D is for Dishes

Stir-fry veggies in a wok.
Wrap seaweed around rice.
Dip long noodles in a broth.
Asian food has lots of spice.

Chinatowns and other ethnic communities are best known for their restaurants. People come from far and wide to taste yummy Asian-inspired dishes. For example, dim sum restaurants in Chinatowns are very popular. Dim sum is a traditional Chinese meal of small plates of dumplings and other bite-size snacks. It is usually eaten with tea. Japanese sushi and ramen noodle houses are also very popular. Other popular Asian foods include Vietnamese pho or noodle soup, Korean barbeque, and even Asian fusion. Asian fusion is the combination of traditional Asian dishes with other cultural dishes. Examples are a kimchi hotdog or a sushi burrito.

Some dishes are Asian American creations. For example, fortune cookies are served at Chinese restaurants but they're not Chinese. They were inspired by a Japanese cracker made with sesame and miso. Japanese immigrants set up bakeries in California and made the cookies with vanilla and butter to suit American tastes. In the 1940s, Chinese American restaurants were more popular than Japanese restaurants, so they offered fortune cookies as a form of dessert. Other Asian American food creations are Chinese chicken salad and the California roll.

A is for

E is for Etiquette

Gathered together for a meal,
family and friends make a toast.
They compliment the cook
and always thank the host.

In many Asian and Asian American cultures, food is the center of family gatherings. Eating "family style" is when food is served on platters meant for sharing, instead of being served on individual plates. This gives everyone a chance to try different things and share meals together.

There is different eating etiquette, or rules, for each Asian culture. But there are some similarities. It is common for elders to eat first. It is common to slurp noodles and bring bowls directly to one's mouth. It is also common to use chopsticks, spoons, and even hands to pick up food. For example, in some Indian customs, the right hand is used to eat, and the left hand is used to pass dishes and serve others.

Many Asian cultures use chopsticks. Chopsticks are used to pick up and cut food. (Knives and forks are not commonly found at Asian meals.) There are special rules for using chopsticks. Chopsticks should not be laid down vertically and should not be pointed at anyone. One end should be used for your mouth and the opposite end should be used to serve food to others.

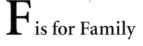

F is for Family

Working together as one,
families take care of each other.
Honor is shared among all:
father, mother, sister, and brother.

The Asian American experience emphasizes tradition and family, so families gather to celebrate holidays, special days, and achievements. In some Asian cultures, one's surname (family name) is often said first. In this way, someone is identified as a member of their family and not as an individual. Pacific Islanders are very family-centered. In order to survive on isolated islands, they have had to share resources, food, child-rearing, and work. Families are the key to their survival.

Many Asian immigrants work in the United States and send money back home to family in their heritage countries. This is an example of filial piety. Filial piety is a duty to care for one's parents and elderly family members. Many Asian immigrant parents make sacrifices to provide for their children. They do this with the expectation that their children will care for them in their old age. Today Asian American youth don't follow filial piety principles as much. They prefer to focus on love as a bond rather than obligation.

Ff

G is for Grandparents

Knowledge from elders
  is a gift that they give.
Family history and traditions
  guide the way we live.

G g

Grandparents serve important roles in Asian American families. In addition to helping with childcare, they often are the link to family histories and heritage cultures. As such, they preserve the culture, language, and traditions by teaching them to their children and grandchildren.

They also serve as the connections to a family's ancestors. The spirits of ancestors are believed to be part of the living world. There are different ways to honor one's ancestors. For example, some Asian American families have shrines where family members gather together and make offerings and/or burn incense. Another way to honor ancestors is by living one's best life. Asian Americans acknowledge the sacrifices and struggles of their ancestors. They show appreciation by attributing their successes to those of their ancestors.

In some Asian languages, maternal and paternal grandparents are given different names. This means they're called different things based on whether they are related to one's mother or father.

Heritage and history months recognize and celebrate the cultures, contributions, and influences of various diverse communities.

May is Asian American and Pacific Islander Heritage and History Month. The month commemorates the May 7, 1843, arrival of the first Japanese immigrant to the United States and the May 10, 1869, completion of the Transcontinental Railroad, which was mainly built by Chinese immigrants. The idea for this month was inspired by Jeanie Jew, a congressional staffer. Her great-grandfather had helped build the railroad and years later was killed in an anti-Asian hate attack. Jew wanted to honor him and other Asian Americans. In the 1970s, she worked with political leaders to pass a bill in Congress for an Asian American week. Future bills extended the week to a month and to an annual recognition.

Starting in the 1990s, the Filipino American National Historical Society led the efforts to establish Filipino American History Month, which is in October. October commemorates the arrival of the first Filipinos, who landed in Morro Bay, California, on October 18, 1587. Even though they didn't settle here, these Filipinos were the first Asians to arrive in the United States. October is also the birth month of Larry Itliong, a Filipino American labor leader.

H is for Heritage and History Month

All year long we should learn about
our cultures and our histories.
The months of May and October
provide us many opportunities.

Duke Kahanamoku

Larry Itliong

Jeanie Jew

Kalpana Chawla

Kristi Yamaguchi

Ii

I is for International Travel

We fly across the seas so
family members can meet.
Learning about one's culture
is fun and really neat.

International travel is a big part of the Asian American experience. It helps Asians and Asian Americans stay connected to each other and to their heritages. Asian family members may travel to the United States to visit their American relatives.

Likewise, many Asian Americans may travel back to their heritage countries. They travel to visit family members and/or they travel to learn more about their heritage. In the 1980s, the South Korean government developed a summer program for the children of Korean emigrants to return to Korea in order to learn about Korean culture, language, and history. Although this program is no longer offered, it has inspired several organizations to host similar summer culture camps.

Asian adoptees are children who are adopted from Asian countries into American homes, often by families who are not of Asian ancestry. The three largest Asian adoptees in the United States come from China, Korea, and Vietnam. It is common for Asian adoptees to travel to their heritage countries to learn more about the culture of their birth parents.

J is for Japanese Anime

There are all kinds of anime,
which started in Japan.
All around the world,
you'll find anime fans.

Anime (/a nuh may/) refers to hand-drawn animation from Japan, from which anime originated. In the 1960s, the first Japanese anime shows released in the United States were *Astro Boy* and *Speed Racer*. This sparked an obsession with Japanese culture. In the 1970s, the first US anime fan club, the Cartoon/Fantasy Organization (C/FO), formed in Los Angeles, California. C/FO members met monthly to watch and discuss anime. This led to the formation of other fan groups. In 1988, Streamline Pictures was one of the first American companies to distribute Japanese anime. This helped grow Japanese anime's popularity, creating a nationwide community of anime fans. At conventions, fans often dress up like their favorite characters, which is called cosplay or costume play. Japanese anime has influenced American cartoons such as *Avatar: The Last Airbender*, the Transformers franchise, and many shows on Cartoon Network.

Along with Japanese manga (comics or graphic novels), Japanese horror movies, and Japanese video games, Japanese anime has increased American awareness of and love for Japanese popular culture. Popular culture, or pop culture, refers to cultural products such as music, art, literature, movies, etc. These products are popular among the majority of people in a culture.

K is for Korean Wave

Once the Korean Wave
hit the US shores,
fans couldn't get enough
and started wanting more!

K k

The Korean Wave is the widespread craze for South Korean pop culture. Like a wave, this love spread out from South Korea to China, Japan, Southeast Asia, and then everywhere else. In the United States, the Korean Wave started in Korean American communities, especially in Los Angeles and New York City. Korean Americans couldn't get enough of South Korean fashion, beauty products, food, movies, television shows (or K-dramas), and pop music (or K-pop). Their love of all things South Korean spread to other Americans as well.

K-pop began in the 1990s when South Koreans became more exposed to American pop music, especially hip-hop, rap, and R&B. Big Bang is a boy band known as the "Kings of K-pop." Their song "Fantastic Baby" was one of the first K-pop songs to strike it big in the United States. In 2017, BTS, another South Korean boy band, became hugely popular. K-pop girl bands, like Blackpink, are also popular. Although K-pop is a South Korean creation, many K-pop bands are writing bilingual songs, including English words in their lyrics.

Many Asian American communities celebrate the Lunar New Year. The Lunar New Year marks the first new moon of the lunisolar calendar, which is based on the 12 full cycles of the moon and is about 354 days long. The actual Lunar New Year's Day falls on a different day every year, typically in late January or early February. Lunar New Year celebrations take place over 15 days and include family reunions, banquets of food, parades with firecrackers, and lion and dragon dances. The San Francisco Chinese New Year Festival and Parade is an annual event. It is the oldest and largest Lunar New Year celebration outside of Asia. It's also the largest Asian cultural event in North America.

Celebrating the Lunar New Year is a tradition in Asian countries such as China, Korea, and Vietnam. However, several Asian countries celebrate it in different ways and at different times. Southeast Asian countries such as Thailand, Laos, Cambodia, and parts of India welcome in the new year in April. The Hmong New Year takes place in the fall, at the end of the harvest season.

Ll

L is for Lunar New Year

A lucky new year would
        bring fortune and wealth.
Everyone also hopes for
happiness and health.

M is for Movements

They fought for equal rights,
  equal treatment, and the like.
A movement could include
  a protest, march, and strike.

Larry Itliong

Philip Vera Cruz

Wong Kim Ark

Grace Lee Boggs

Yuri Kochiyama

M m

Asian Americans and Pacific Islanders have a history of working for social change in the United States. This includes fighting for citizenship rights, equal pay, or the right to not be bullied because of race. In 1898, Wong Kim Ark, a son of Chinese immigrants, fought for his right to be an American citizen based on his being born in San Francisco. The US Supreme Court agreed, establishing that citizenship is based on one's place of birth.

There have been many examples of Asian American activism. For example, in 1965, Larry Itliong and Philip Vera Cruz, Filipino labor leaders, led a strike to get better wages and working conditions for farm-workers. In 1969, a group of multiracial student activists led a campus strike to fight for ethnic studies programs in schools. In 1982, the murder of Vincent Chin inspired Asian American communities to stand in solidarity. Asian American movements continue today. Activists are fighting against anti-Asian hate. They are fighting to be seen and heard.

N n

Spelling bee contestants
first compete at their schools.
They study and practice,
not wanting to lose.

In 1925, nine newspapers joined together to host a national spelling bee. Today, this event continues on as the National Spelling Bee, which takes place every year and is televised on ESPN. About 11 million students participate. They compete in several rounds and the champions win cash prizes and other gifts.

Over the past several years, the majority of the spelling bee champions have been Indian Americans. Indian Americans have turned the spelling bee into a highly competitive sport. This started in 1985, when Balu Natarajan became the first Indian American to win the National Spelling Bee. He became a source of pride for the Indian American community.

For some Indian Americans, competing in spelling bees is a highly respected activity, and parents invest a lot of time and resources toward it. They pay for spelling bee coaches, set up tutoring centers, and create study materials. They also host regional and national spelling competitions to provide opportunities for practice. They quiz their children for several hours a day. In this way, practicing for the bee is a family event.

58th Annual
RIPPS HOW
onal Spelli e
1985

68
CHICAGO
IL

Asian Americans are out of this world! In 1985, Ellison S. Onizuka became the first Asian American astronaut to fly in space on the space shuttle *Discovery*. This was America's first classified manned military spaceflight. Onizuka first started as a pilot for the United States Air Force. He was the first Japanese American selected to participate in NASA's Space Shuttle program. Sadly, in 1986, Onizuka died in the *Challenger* space shuttle disaster.

Sunita Williams is an Indian American astronaut. She formerly held the records for the most spacewalks by a woman (seven) and most spacewalk time for a woman (50 hours, 40 minutes). In 2007, Williams completed the Boston Marathon while running on a treadmill on the International Space Station, becoming the first person to complete a marathon in space.

In addition to space flight, Asian Americans have made significant achievements in aviation. For example, in 1932, Katherine Sui Fun Cheung became the first Asian American woman to earn a pilot's license. She was famous for performing tricks in the air.

Oo

O is for Outer Space

From astronauts to aviators,
they launched from Earth, home base.
These brave Americans made their mark,
and flew to outer space.

P is for Pioneers

As the firsts in many fields,
pioneers blazed trails in the past,
paving the way for others
to ensure they're not the last.

Victoria Manalo Draves

Dalip Singh Saund

Patsy Mink

Kamala Harris

Sunisa Lee

Anna May Wong

Wataru Misaka

Sessue Hayakawa

There have been many Asian American pioneers in various fields, from politics to sports to Hollywood.

Asian American politicians have fought for better laws and policies. In 1956, Dalip Singh Saund became the first Asian American to serve as a US representative. He was the first Indian American and first Sikh to serve in Congress. In 1964, Patsy Mink became the first woman of color to serve as a US representative and the first Asian American woman to serve in Congress. In 1972, she became the first Asian American to run for US president. In 2021, Kamala Harris, as vice president, became the highest-ranking Asian American politician in United States history. Harris is half-Indian and half-Black.

Asian American pioneers have made high scores in sports. In 1947, Wataru Misaka was the first person of color to play American professional basketball. He played for the New York Knicks. In 1948, Victoria Manalo Draves, a half-Filipina diver, was the first Asian American Olympic champion. In 2020, Sunisa Lee became the first Hmong American Olympian.

There were Asian American pioneers in Hollywood. Anna May Wong was the first Chinese American film star. Sessue Hayakawa was the first Asian American to be a leading man.

Q is for Queen Lili'uokalani

Queen Lili'uokalani of Hawai'i
didn't rule for very long.
But she still made an impact
and wrote Hawai'i's national song.

Queen Lili'uokalani (/luh lee uh wow kuh laa nee/), born Lydia Kamaka'eha, lived from 1838 to 1917. In 1891, she became the first woman to rule Hawai'i. She was also the last ruler of the Hawaiian kingdom when the United States made Hawai'i into a state. This took away Lili'uokalani's power. She peacefully fought for a free Hawai'i until her death. Today, some activists are still fighting for Hawaiian independence.

Before she was queen, Lili'uokalani was a gifted student of music. She could play several instruments, including the piano, organ, ukulele, guitar, and zither. In 1866, she wrote Hawai'i's national song. The song was called "He Mele Lāhui Hawai'i," which means "The Song of the Hawaiian Nation." This brought a sense of pride to the Hawaiian people. Her song was used at official events, replacing the British song "God Save the King." (In 1876, when her brother became king, he replaced her song with one of his own.) This song was her first publication. She ended up writing more than 150 songs. Her most popular song is "Aloha 'Oe," which she wrote in 1878. This song, which means "Farewell to Thee," is still sung today.

Q q

R is for Remembrance

A Day of Remembrance
means "never forget."
Mistakes from the past
bring shame and regret.

R r

On February 19, 1942, President Franklin D. Roosevelt signed Executive Order (EO) 9066, which forced the incarceration of all Americans of Japanese ancestry during World War II. About 120,000 Japanese Americans were removed from their homes on the West Coast and sent to incarceration camps. This was done to protect national security after Japan bombed Pearl Harbor in Hawai'i. None of the incarcerated Japanese Americans were found to be disloyal.

On November 25, 1978, activists from the Japanese American Citizens League (JACL) observed the first Day of Remembrance in Washington state. Since then, the day has moved to February 19 as a reminder of the day Roosevelt signed the order to incarcerate Japanese Americans. People recognize February 19 as a day to commemorate the people affected by EO 9066 and activists such as Fred Korematsu who resisted EO 9066. They continue to raise public awareness about the Japanese Incarceration experience.

The JACL and other activist groups continue to fight for justice. They demand that Congress pay the camp survivors for each day they were imprisoned.

As painful as it is to look at this history, it's important to remember it so actions like these can never happen again.

Some Asian parents worry about their American-born children losing their Asian heritage. So they send their Asian American children to American schools during the week and then to Saturday Schools on the weekend. These Saturday Schools offer language classes and classes covering topics such as dance, music, art, crafts, and other cultural activities. They usually take place in rented spaces at local schools or churches. Most take place on Saturdays, but some heritage schools take place on Sundays or after school during the week.

The most common Saturday Schools are the Mandarin Chinese and Cantonese Chinese heritage schools. But there are many other heritage schools that teach Japanese, Korean, Tagalog, and other Asian languages. Organized by community leaders, they are usually located in areas with a large number of Asian Americans.

Non-Asian students also attend these Saturday Schools as more parents are seeing the value of being bilingual and of being able to speak an Asian language in today's global economy. In some schools, classes in Chinese and Japanese are offered.

S is for Saturday Schools

It's hard waking up early
on Saturday for school.
But speaking a heritage
language is a valuable tool.

T is for Tea

With its tea, milk, and ice,
plus, tapioca so gummy,
bubble tea is a treat.
Slurp it up—it's yummy!

Tt

Tea originated in China and was traded along a network of ancient trade routes known as the Silk Road. This is how tea spread out to the world. There are many types of tea and many ceremonies and rituals around the preparing and drinking of tea.

Bubble tea, as it's called on the East Coast, or boba tea, as it's called on the West Coast, is a very popular tea drink. It was created in Taiwan in the 1980s. It is a combination of tea, milk, and "bubbles." The bubbles refer to the foam that forms when shaking the milk tea. They also refer to the little balls, made of anything from tapioca to fruit jelly. These bubbles are also called boba or pearls. Bubble tea drinks can be served with or without milk, ice, sugar, and various toppings. They can also be served in various forms, such as a slush or punch.

Bubble tea spread from Taiwan to Chinatowns overseas. In the United States, Taiwanese immigrants opened boba or bubble tea shops in Los Angeles. Today, bubble tea shops can be found almost everywhere. These are just like coffeehouses—public spaces where people, especially Asian Americans, can meet and hang out.

U is for Undefeated Spirit

Serving their country, risking their lives—
these soldiers were loyal and true.
Fighting for the United States,
they were Americans through and through.

Asian Americans have shown their patriotism and undefeated spirit by proudly serving in the US military, even though they were often treated unfairly.

For example, Japanese American men, many of whom were sent to incarceration camps during World War II, formed the 442nd Regimental Combat Team. This team is the most highly decorated combat unit in American military history.

In 1942, Filipino battalions, made up of Americans of Filipino ancestry and resident Filipinos, were formed. They served alongside US Army soldiers fighting against the Japanese who were attacking the Philippines.

There are many other Asian American military heroes. In 1944, Hazel Ying Lee became the first Chinese American woman to fly for the US military. Having served in World War II and the Korean War, Kurt Chew-Een Lee was the first Asian American US Marine Corps officer. Tammy Duckworth, US senator, was one of the first women to fly army combat missions during the Iraq War. While flying a helicopter, she was hit and lost her legs and partial use of her right arm.

This proud tradition of military service continues today.

U u

V is for Vietnam Veterans Memorial

To remember fallen soldiers,
    Maya Lin designed a wall.
People come to visit;
    they look for names, honoring all.

Beginning in the mid-1950s the Vietnam War was fought between the Communist government of North Vietnam against South Vietnam and the United States. It lasted close to 20 years and resulted in the deaths of millions of people. Because of this war, many Southeast Asians—including Vietnamese, Cambodian, Hmong, Laotian, and Thai people—were forced to flee, immigrating to the United States as refugees.

In 1982, the Vietnam Veterans Memorial was unveiled in Washington, D.C. The memorial includes the Three Servicemen statue, the Vietnam Women's Memorial statue, the In Memory plaque, and the Memorial Wall. The names of more than 58,000 American men and women killed or missing in the Vietnam War are inscribed on the wall. The "wall" is made up of two sections, each measuring more than 200 feet. It was designed by a 21-year-old college student named Maya Lin. Lin, a Chinese American, entered a competition to design the memorial. She wanted to honor all those who suffered in the Vietnam War. She said, "I wanted something that would simply say . . . 'They should be remembered.' "

W is for Writers

The Asian American experience
needs to be widely shared and told.
When our storytellers create,
amazing stories can unfold.

"Talk Story" is a native Hawaiian expression meaning "to chat informally." It is a story-telling style steeped in oral traditions, myths, and personal experiences. With stories, people share their cultures and histories, passing down knowledge from one generation to another.

Asian American writers document the Asian American experience. Yone Noguchi, a Japanese American, was one of the first Asian American poets. He is famous for writing poems about Yosemite. Carlos Bulosan is famous for writing about his Filipino American experience in *America is in the Heart*. Amy Tan (*The Joy Luck Club*) and Maxine Hong Kingston (*The Woman Warrior*) are Chinese American authors who helped popularize Asian American literature.

Asian American playwrights have made significant contributions. David Henry Hwang, a Chinese American, has won many awards. He wrote *M. Butterfly*, which was the first Asian American play to be produced on Broadway.

Asian Americans have told stories in different ways. There are news reporters such as Connie Chung and Lisa Ling, who are both Chinese Americans. There are movie creators such as Filipino American Destin Cretton, who directed *Shang-Chi and the Legend of the Ten Rings*.

Ronald Takaki

Yone Noguchi

Carlos Bulosan

Amy Tan

Maxine Hong Kingston

Frank Chin

David Henry Hwang

Connie Chung

Lisa Ling

Lulu Wang

Jon M. Chu

Justin Lin

Ang Lee

X Marks the Martial Arts Move

Born in the year of the dragon,
Bruce Lee was fiery and quick.
His strong stance and clear mind
helped power a punch and a kick.

Martial arts are traditional Asian forms of combat focused on physical, mental, and spiritual development. In the early 1900s, American businessmen traveling in Japan were introduced to judo, a Japanese martial art. They asked judo masters such as Yamashita Yoshitsugu to come to the United States to teach. Yoshitsugu taught rich, famous Americans, including President Theodore Roosevelt, who became America's first brown belt. Roosevelt encouraged military soldiers to train in the martial arts.

It was Bruce Lee who made martial arts popular to all Americans. Born in San Francisco in 1940, Lee was a Chinese American movie star and martial artist. He created and taught a style called "Jeet Kune Do" or "The Way of the Intercepting Fist." This style combined kung fu, boxing, and fencing. Its goal is to intercept an attack with another attack. Lee's motto was to "be like water." He was a pioneer in the mixed martial arts.

Other Asian martial arts such as karate and tai chi are practiced in the United States. Yoga, which has also become popular in the United States, is a Hindu spiritual practice including breath control, meditation, and postures.

Xx

Y is for Yahoo and YouTube

Our lives have greatly improved
due to tech breakthroughs.
With clicks and finger swipes,
we access info and video views.

Yy

There is no doubt that technology and the Internet have changed our lives. Asian Americans have made many inventions and innovations in the Internet industry.

Before Google, there was Yahoo. Yahoo was a pioneer in search engines. It created the first web directory, which is an online list of websites. It invented many apps and services that we still use today. Jerry Yang, a Taiwanese American, is the co-founder of Yahoo. While studying at Stanford University in 1994, he met David Filo and they created an Internet website called "Jerry and David's Guide to the World Wide Web." This became Yahoo.

YouTube is a free online video-sharing website. It was invented in 2005 by Chad Hurley, Steve Chen, and Jawed Karim. Steve Chen is a Taiwanese American computer scientist and businessman. Jawed Karim is an American software engineer who is half-Bangladeshi.

Wong Fu Productions is a filmmaking group and one of the original trailblazers of Asian American YouTubers. It was founded by Wesley Chan, Ted Fu, and Philip Wang.

The Chinese zodiac is a system of Asian astrology that is based on the lunar calendar, whereas Western astrology is based on the constellations. The Chinese zodiac is divided into a 12-year cycle with a different animal representing each year. The animals are rat, ox, tiger, rabbit, dragon, snake, horse, goat, monkey, rooster, dog, and pig. The Chinese zodiac has influenced other cultural zodiacs, with differences in animal names and myths. Other Asian countries with zodiacs include Korea, Japan, Vietnam, Cambodia, Thailand, Nepal, and Mongolia. A common theme with all the zodiacs is the belief in luck, which is determined by one's zodiac sign.

Americans tend to believe that individuals make their own luck, whereas Asians focus more on family and community. Today's Asian Americans may not believe in the zodiac as a sign of their fate. But they still celebrate the cultural aspects of the zodiac. They turn to astrology, both Eastern and Western, for fun.

Asian Americans tend to be less religious than other Americans. Instead, they believe in this idea that there is something greater than themselves out there. The zodiac is just an example of a greater power. But there are Asian American groups that practice organized religion.

Z is for Zodiac

We celebrate our zodiac signs
once every twelve years.
These animals tell our fortunes,
and help calm any fears.

Concepts and Words To Know

Activists: people who fight for political or social change to improve the lives of others

Ancestors: people who were in someone's family in past times; people from whom a person is descended

Angel Island Immigration Station: a place located in San Francisco Bay where immigrants from Asia were held, processed, and either allowed to enter the United States or sent back to where they came from

African American civil rights movement: an organized effort from the 1940s to the 1960s led by Black Americans to end racial discrimination and gain equal rights under the law

Emigrants: people who leave one country or region to live in another country or region

Ethnic studies: courses and programs that study the history and experiences of racial groups in the United States

Heritage countries: the countries from which immigrants and/or their families originally came from

Immigrants: people who move to a new country

Incarceration: the state of being forced into confinement in a jail or prison

Naturalized citizens: people who are born in another country but who have lawfully become citizens of their new country

Refugees: people who seek a safe haven after being forced to flee violence, persecution, or war

Solidarity: a feeling or condition of unity based on common goals

The Transcontinental Railroad: a train line that crossed the United States, connecting the Pacific coast to the Atlantic coast

Resources:

The Asian American Education Project (https://asianamericanedu.org) provides free lesson plans and resources about APIDA history and culture.

The Center for Asian American Media (https://caamedia.org) hosts film festivals and produces media content dedicated to presenting APIDA stories and experiences.

The Chinese Historical Society of America (https://chsa.org) provides exhibitions, publications, and programs that promote the contributions and legacy of the Chinese in America.

Desis Rising Up & Moving (DRUM) (https://www.drumnyc.org) mobilizes and empowers South Asian immigrants to lead social and policy changes.

The Japanese American National Museum (https://www.janm.org) provides exhibitions, programs, documentaries, and curriculum about Japanese American history.

The National Park Service created a list of notable Asian American and Pacific Islander historic locations on this website: https://www.nps.gov/subjects/aapiheritage/places.htm

PBS's *Asian Americans* (https://www.pbs.org/weta/asian-americans/) is a documentary series that examines the history and impact of Asian Americans.

The Smithsonian Asian Pacific American Center (https://smithsonianapa.org) provides museum experiences that feature APIDA history, art, and culture. It offers collections, exhibits, cultural festivals, public programs, research, and job opportunities.

Stop AAPI Hate (https://stopaapihate.org) is a reporting center that collects and provides data about violence against APIDA communities.

The Southeast Asia Resource Action Center (https://www.searac.org) provides leadership and community development programs in an effort to empower Cambodian, Laotian, and Vietnamese American communities, especially refugees.

Activities

OCTOBER
Filipinx American History Month

ACTIVITY 1   Larry Itliong, a Filipino American labor activist, fought for farmworkers' rights. Learn more about Itliong and the Delano grape strike. Make a timeline including visuals and captions of the causes and effects of the strike.

ACTIVITY 2   Listen to Filipino American musicians. Some examples are Bruno Mars, Olivia Rodrigo, H.E.R., and Ruby Ibarra. Examine how their Filipino backgrounds impact their music.

ACTIVITY 3   Learn about Pacita Abad, a Filipina American artist. She is known for her colorful and textured paintings. Create your own painting inspired by her use of circles, lines, and found objects.

ACTIVITY 4   Cook a traditional Filipino dish that is still eaten by many Filipino Americans. Ensaladang Mangga is a yummy salad that is easy to make. Cut up mangoes, tomatoes, red onions, and cilantro. Make a dressing with vinegar, fish sauce, oil, sugar, and pepper. Mix everything together.

ACTIVITY 5   Big wooden spoons and forks can be found hanging on the walls of many Filipino and Filipino American homes. They're symbols of health, prosperity, and pride. Learn more about this tradition. Then get a wooden spoon and decorate it. Hang the finished product on your wall.

MAY
Asian Pacific Islander Desi American History/Heritage Month

ACTIVITY 1   Learn more about your local Chinatown. Visit it in person or online. Take in all the sights and sounds. Create a brochure including fun facts about its history and places to see.

ACTIVITY 2   Sriracha is a type of hot sauce. It's often used in Southeast Asia. Learn more about David Tran, who made sriracha popular in the United States. Make a list of how sriracha is currently being used. Then, create your own recipe using sriracha.

ACTIVITY 3   Write a list of movies or TV shows featuring Asian Americans. Make a video trailer or poster to promote the movie or TV show.

ACTIVITY 4   *Hula* is the Hawaiian word for "dance." This traditional Pacific Islander dance is characterized by its slow and graceful movements of the hips and hands. Learn how to hula by watching videos or hiring a dance teacher.

ACTIVITY 5   Rangoli art consists of patterns that are created on floors or tabletops using colored powder. Learn more about this traditional Indian art form that is still practiced by some Indian Americans. Make your own version of rangoli art. Create or print a geometric pattern. Outline all the lines with glue. Put salt on the glue. Shake out the excess salt and wait for the glue to dry. Apply watercolors and watch the colors come to life.

This book is dedicated to all the students, faculty, staff, and community members who have supported SDSU's APIDA Center.

—Virginia

For my family in Japan, Hawaii, and California, who always make me proud to be Japanese American

—Tracy

SLEEPING BEAR PRESS™

2395 South Huron Parkway, Suite 200, Ann Arbor, MI 48104
www.sleepingbearpress.com
© Sleeping Bear Press
Printed and bound in the United States.

10 9 8 7 6 5 4 3 2

Library of Congress Cataloging-in-Publication Data
Names: Loh-Hagan, Virginia, author. | Bishop, Tracy Nishimura, illustrator.
Title: A is for Asian American : an Asian Pacific Islander Desi American
alphabet / by Virginia Loh-Hagan ; and illustrated by Tracy Nishimura Bishop.
Other titles: Asian Pacific Islander Desi American alphabet
Description: Ann Arbor, MI : Sleeping Bear Press, [2022] | Audience: Ages
6-10 | Audience: Grades 2-3 | Summary: "Following the alphabet, poetry
and expository text explain and showcase the cultural traditions and
contributions of Asian Americans throughout U.S. history. Topics include
traditions in food, family, and social celebrations, as well as key
moments in history and milestone achievements"-- Provided by publisher.
Identifiers: LCCN 2022003570 | ISBN 9781534111370 (hardcover)
Subjects: LCSH: Asian Americans--Social life and customs--Juvenile
literature. | Asian Americans--History--Juvenile literature. | United
States--Civilization--Asian influences. | English
language--Alphabet--Juvenile literature. | Alphabet books--Juvenile literature.
Classification: LCC E184.A75 L583 2022 | DDC 973/.0495--dc23/eng/20220225
LC record available at https://lccn.loc.gov/2022003570